Eleanor Roosevelt

History Maker Bios

Mary Winget

BARNES
&NOBLE
BOOKS
NEW YORK

To Audrey, another remarkable woman

Illustrations by Tim Parlin

Text copyright © 2003 by Lerner Publications Company
Illustrations copyright © 2003 by Lerner Publications Company

This edition published by Barnes & Noble, Inc.,
by arrangement with Lerner Publications Company,
a division of Lerner Publishing Group, Minneapolis, MN.

2003 Barnes & Noble Books

ISBN: 0-7607-3601-4

Printed in China

11 10 9 8 7 6 5 4 3 2

TABLE OF CONTENTS

INTRODUCTION

Eleanor Roosevelt cared deeply about other people. Throughout her life, she worked to make things better for poor and disadvantaged people. As First Lady, the wife of President Franklin Delano Roosevelt, she was active in politics. After her years in the White House, she worked for world peace.

Some people thought Eleanor should stay home and mind her own business. But most people loved her. By the end of her life, she had been voted America's "Most Admired Woman."

This is her story.

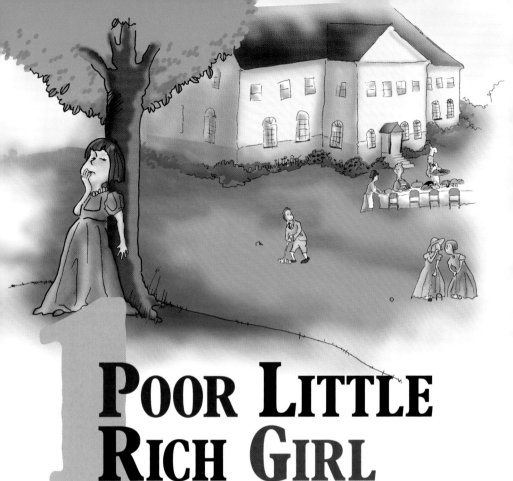

1 POOR LITTLE RICH GIRL

Anna Eleanor Roosevelt was born into a rich New York family on October 11, 1884. Her father, Elliott, was thrilled with his baby girl. But Eleanor's mother, Anna Hall Roosevelt, was disappointed. Anna was one of the most beautiful ladies in New York. Little Eleanor was plain looking.

She was such a shy and serious child that Anna began calling her Granny. Anna didn't think Eleanor would ever fit in.

Eleanor was happiest when she was with her father. She especially looked forward to Thanksgiving, when he took her to serve dinner to homeless boys. He tried to help poor people whenever he could. But Elliott was often away from home. He also had a drinking problem. When he was drinking, everything changed. He even forgot promises he had made to Eleanor.

Elliott Roosevelt called his daughter a "miracle from heaven." Eleanor missed him terribly when they were apart.

When Eleanor was eight years old, her mother caught a terrible disease called diphtheria and died. Eleanor and her two little brothers, Ellie and Hall, went to live with Grandmother Hall, Anna's mother, in her big house in New York City.

Every summer, they moved to a house near Tivoli, in upstate New York. The children had fun there. They played secret games, caught tadpoles in the little stream, and sat outside and read. Sometimes they visited Uncle Ted and his family on Long Island. Uncle Ted, Theodore Roosevelt, was Elliott's brother.

Uncle Ted loved the outdoors. He and his lively family were great athletes.

Eleanor poses with her horse. She enjoyed horseback riding and jumping at her grandmother's home in Tivoli.

Eleanor's brother Ellie died in 1893. Then, during the summer of 1894, her father died. Nine-year-old Eleanor was so sad, she cried herself to sleep. She had loved her father more than anyone.

When Eleanor was fourteen, she went to her first party with boys. Grandmother Hall dressed Eleanor in a short white dress—a little girl's dress. The other girls, including her cousin Alice, wore beautiful long gowns. Even so, a distant cousin asked Eleanor to dance. His name was Franklin Delano Roosevelt. For Eleanor, he saved the day.

At Allenswood, Eleanor and her classmates learned good manners. Eleanor is in the back row, third from right.

In the fall of 1899, Grandmother Hall sent fifteen-year-old Eleanor to Allenswood, a girls' school near London, England. Eleanor felt at home at Allenswood. Mademoiselle Marie Souvestre ran the school. She took a special liking to Eleanor and encouraged her to trust herself. At Allenswood, Eleanor made many friends. She learned to ask questions and to enjoy learning.

Eleanor returned to New York during the summer of 1902. That fall, she sometimes met her cousin Franklin for tea. The two cousins enjoyed talking to each other.

Around the same time, Grandmother Hall decided it was time for Eleanor's "coming out." When wealthy young women became adults, they celebrated with a year of fancy parties and dances. Shy Eleanor was unhappy going to parties. To make matters worse, her Uncle Ted had recently become the president of the United States. As the niece of the president, she was in the spotlight.

Eleanor's photo was taken for her "coming out." She worried that she was not as beautiful as her mother had been.

Like many poor Americans, this mother and her young children worked long hours. They are making artificial flowers.

Eleanor knew that most people in New York City did not lead such glamorous lives. Poor people crowded into unsafe, dirty apartments. Many children went hungry. Disease spread easily. And some workers—men, women, and children— worked more than twelve hours a day in dangerous places. They earned little money. Eleanor thought this was unfair.

Eleanor joined other young, wealthy women who wanted to improve life for the poor. She taught exercise and dance classes to poor children. She worked to make factories and stores safe for workers.

Eleanor liked her work. It made her feel close to her father, who had taught her to help the poor. But Eleanor realized she wanted to do more than help. She wanted to change the way things were.

Eleanor's life was already changing. She and Franklin had been writing letters to each other, and he often visited her. In October he asked her to marry him. The wedding took place on March 17, 1905, Saint Patrick's Day.

UNCLE TED STEALS THE SHOW

Eleanor and Franklin's wedding was exciting for the guests, but not because of the bride and groom. Uncle Ted, still the president of the United States, gave the bride away. After the wedding service, the guests forgot about Eleanor and Franklin. They gathered around the president to hear his lively stories. Eleanor and Franklin finally decided they, too, would join the party.

Like many wealthy couples, Eleanor and Franklin spent their honeymoon in Europe. They stopped in San Remo, Italy.

As Franklin's wife, Eleanor behaved like other rich married women. She stopped her work with the poor and spent time at home.

In 1906, Eleanor gave birth to a baby girl, Anna Eleanor. Eleanor didn't know much about babies, so she hired a nurse to help. The family grew quickly. James was born in 1907. Elliott came along in 1910.

Franklin had been working at a law firm in New York, but he wanted to get into politics. In 1910, he ran for the state senate as a Democrat and won the election. The family moved to Albany, the state capital.

In 1913, the family moved to Washington, D.C. Franklin had been asked to work for the new president, Woodrow Wilson. In Washington, Eleanor did what other wives of politicians did. She felt shy, but she visited other wives every day. On Wednesdays she stayed home to receive guests. She and Franklin went to countless parties.

Eleanor tried to take good care of her children—Anna, James, Elliott, and by this time, Franklin Jr. and John. She read to them every night. She sent them to the best schools. Like her Grandmother Hall, she was strict. Being a mother was hard work.

Eleanor and Franklin hold the first two of their five children, Anna (RIGHT) and James (LEFT).

Franklin's mind was on other things. The nations of Europe were fighting in World War I. Franklin had to make sure the United States could defend itself. In the spring of 1917, the United States joined the war.

In July, Franklin visited troops fighting in Europe. He came home in September, sick with double pneumonia. While she was unpacking Franklin's luggage, Eleanor found love letters to Franklin. They were from Lucy Mercer, Eleanor's own friend and secretary. Eleanor realized that Franklin was in love with Lucy.

Franklin agreed to stop seeing Lucy. He and Eleanor decided to stay married. But Eleanor felt sad and hurt. She lost her self-confidence. Eleanor realized that her life had changed. And she decided to change, too.

2 A POLITICAL WOMAN

Eleanor slowly began to take charge of her life. She grew more independent about raising her children. She also voted for the first time. Congress passed the Nineteenth Amendment on August 26, 1919. The amendment gave women the right to vote. Eleanor began to think about getting involved in politics.

Eleanor (SEATED) was the only woman on Franklin's campaign trip.

In 1920, Franklin ran for vice president. James Cox was running for president. Franklin asked Eleanor to campaign with him on a four-week train trip. Franklin made the same speech at every stop— except that it kept getting longer. When Eleanor thought it was time for Franklin to stop talking, she yanked his coattails.

Franklin and James Cox lost the election, so Eleanor and Franklin went home to New York. Eleanor began to work on her own activities, separate from Franklin's.

She joined a new organization, the League of Women Voters. The women in the league wanted to make the most of their right to vote. They wanted the government to improve life for poor workers, women, and children.

Eleanor met new friends through the league. Her new friends were different from her aunts and cousins. Instead of spending their time going to ladies' lunches and teas, they had jobs. They were independent and well educated. They encouraged Eleanor to think for herself.

During the 1920s, Eleanor (RIGHT) began to get more involved in politics. Here, she is on her way to a U.S. Senate hearing.

During the summer of 1921, tragedy struck Eleanor's family. Franklin developed an illness called polio. He was paralyzed from the waist down. No one knew if he would ever be able to walk again.

Eventually Franklin was well enough to work again. But he wasn't able to walk. He had to use a wheelchair to get around.

Louis Howe, Franklin's most important assistant, hoped that Franklin would return to politics. In the meantime, he wanted voters to remember Franklin. He asked Eleanor to keep the Roosevelt name known to the public.

Franklin tried to regain his strength by swimming. He often went to Warm Springs, Georgia, to swim in the hot springs there.

Eleanor wasn't sure how she could do that, but she wanted to be useful. So Eleanor worked harder to change things. She decided to join the Women's Trade Union League, which fought for better working conditions for women. She even agreed to make her first public speech.

ELEANOR COMES OUT OF HER SHELL

Before Eleanor made her first public speech, she felt very worried about speaking to a large group. She spoke in a high voice and sometimes let out nervous giggles. Louis Howe coached her. He helped her decide what to say. He reminded her to take deep breaths and smile. He told her, "Have something to say, say it, and then sit down." Eleanor realized that if she wanted to be useful, she had to overcome her shyness. She soon became a popular speaker.

In 1927, Eleanor and two friends bought Todhunter School, a private school for girls in New York City. Eleanor taught history, literature, and current events. She took her students to courthouses, markets, and slums—places they would not otherwise see. Like Marie Souvestre had done for her, Eleanor opened the world for her students.

In 1928, Franklin ran for governor of New York and won the election. The Roosevelts again moved to Albany. Eleanor continued teaching and making speeches.

Together with her friends Marian Dickerman (MIDDLE) and Nancy Cook (RIGHT), Eleanor bought Todhunter School. Marian was the school's principal.

During the 1932 presidential campaign, Eleanor and Franklin make a stop in Savanna, Illinois.

Eleanor also helped Franklin. He couldn't get around easily, so she became his legs. She went places he couldn't go. She inspected state prisons and hospitals and told Franklin what she saw there.

In 1932, Franklin was nominated for president. Secretly, Eleanor did not want Franklin to become president. She thought she would have to give up her own work. Still, Eleanor helped Franklin's campaign. She organized the women of the Democratic Party. Eleanor also campaigned with Franklin around the country.

Jobless people gathered at employment agencies in hopes of finding work during the Great Depression.

On their travels, Eleanor and Franklin saw how the Great Depression, a long period of hard times, was affecting the country. Many factories and businesses were closed. Thousands of people were out of work. Many had lost their homes. People stood in long lines to get food. Something had to be done.

On election night, Eleanor greeted thousands of supporters in the ballroom of the Biltmore Hotel in New York. Franklin waited upstairs for the election returns to come in. Soon it became clear. Voters had chosen Franklin Delano Roosevelt for their president. Whether she wanted to or not, Eleanor was about to become the First Lady of the United States of America.

3 ELEANOR EVERYWHERE

A t first Eleanor wasn't sure what her role as First Lady would be. Most First Ladies stayed out of politics. They didn't talk to reporters. They hosted parties and entertained guests. They left the nation's business to their husbands. But Eleanor was interested in politics. She wanted to be useful—to Franklin and to the causes she supported.

Franklin was sworn in as president on March 4, 1933. Two days later, Eleanor held a press conference. It was the first time a First Lady had ever done that. She invited only female reporters. They talked about child labor and other social issues.

Franklin was busy putting his New Deal programs together. The New Deal was his plan to help people and get the country out of the depression. Eleanor was busy, too. She had her own ideas about helping people. She wrote a book called *It's Up to Women.* It suggested ways that women could help the nation. She also started her own radio show.

Eleanor speaks on the radio. Some people called her the "First Lady of the Radio."

Eleanor often took trips around the country. Wherever she went, she saw how people suffered during the depression. She was especially shocked by conditions in coal mining towns of West Virginia. The coal mines had closed, and there was no other work for the miners. Many families had lost their homes and were living in tents. Children were hungry and sick.

Eleanor wanted to help. She worked to find homes, jobs, food, health care, and education for 125 of the poor West Virginia families. Eleanor helped start a new town, Arthurdale. Her work there inspired people to build similar communities across the country.

Eleanor visits Arthurdale, the West Virginia town she helped build.

Eleanor set up camps that provided work for unemployed women. She spoke at this camp in Bear Mountain, New York.

Eleanor had become a voice for the poor and the weak. People wrote to her about their problems. In one year, she received more than 300,000 letters.

In 1935 Eleanor began to write a daily newspaper column called "My Day." She wrote about social problems, life at the White House, and places she had gone. She continued her women's press conferences.

By 1936, the country was recovering from the Great Depression. Most Americans liked Franklin's New Deal programs. He won reelection to the presidency.

Sometimes Eleanor took on causes that Franklin could not openly support. Eleanor knew that many African Americans were poor. In many parts of the country, they couldn't live, work, or go to school in the same places as white people. Often they were not allowed to vote. Eleanor believed that this was wrong.

ELEANOR AND MARIAN

In 1939 a group called the Daughters of the American Revolution (DAR) refused to let the famous African American singer Marian Anderson perform at a hall they owned in Washington, D.C. They did not want a black person singing there. Eleanor was a member of the DAR. She got angry. She quit the DAR and moved the concert to the Lincoln Memorial. Seventy-five thousand people came to hear Anderson sing. The concert was a success, and Eleanor had taken a public stand for equal rights for African Americans.

Some Americans disapproved of Eleanor's support of equality for all. They were shocked by this picture of Eleanor exchanging flowers with an African American girl.

Franklin knew that many people disagreed with Eleanor. He did not want to make them angry, but he never stood in Eleanor's way. Eleanor was not afraid. She worked to create jobs, safe housing, and voting rights for African Americans.

Eleanor was more active in the country's business than any other First Lady in history. Some politicians and journalists wished Eleanor would keep her ideas to herself. But Eleanor knew she had important work to do.

4 THE WORLD AT WAR

By 1940, much of Europe and Asia was involved in World War II. The United States did not want to go to war, but the country began to prepare—just in case.

Franklin was reelected again in 1940. He was the first president to be elected to a third term. If the United States went to war, the people wanted Franklin to be their leader.

In 1941, the United States joined the fighting. As always, Eleanor found a way to help her country. She went to military bases where soldiers were waiting to go to battle in Europe or Asia. At first the men were surprised to see the First Lady. But she made them feel at ease, and they enjoyed talking with her. She wrote down the names and addresses of their families so she could write to them when she returned home.

Eleanor visits women serving in a special division of the air force at a base in New York.

Franklin saw how helpful Eleanor was. He asked her to travel to the South Pacific to meet U.S. troops there. The important officers in the Pacific didn't want Eleanor to come. But once she got there, they changed their minds. Eleanor helped raise the spirits of the soldiers. She paid special attention to each and every soldier she met.

Instead of eating with important officers, Eleanor ate with ordinary soldiers during her trip to the South Pacific.

Women at War

Eleanor believed that the war could not be won without the help of American women. In the fall of 1942, Eleanor went to England to see how women were helping there. She saw women cooking, working as nurses, flying planes, working in factories, and repairing trucks. Eleanor tried to use some of those ideas at home. She encouraged American women to take jobs building airplanes, ships, and other things needed for the war. She visited women who were serving in special units of the armed forces. Eleanor also helped mothers find care for their children during the workday.

Franklin won his fourth presidential election in 1944. In January 1945, when the war was almost over, he met with world leaders in the Soviet Union to talk about plans for after the war. Franklin hoped an international group—the United Nations—could be formed to promote world peace.

When Franklin came home, he went to Warm Springs, Georgia, for a rest. Eleanor thought he needed it, since he had not been feeling well. Eleanor stayed behind in Washington. On April 12, while attending a charity event, Eleanor got a phone call from the White House. Franklin was dead.

Eleanor called Vice President Harry S. Truman. She asked him to come to the White House quickly so he could be sworn in as president. She also sent a message to her sons. She told them that their Pa had slipped away. "He did his job to the end, as he would want you to do," she said.

Eleanor was sixty years old. She and Franklin had been married for forty years. They had spent the last twelve years in the White House, at the center of world affairs. Without Franklin, Eleanor felt empty.

5 ON HER OWN

With Franklin gone, Eleanor decided to move to an apartment in New York City. She didn't know exactly what she wanted to do. But she knew she did not want to stop trying to make a difference.

Eleanor soon found a way to be useful. President Truman asked her to help form the United Nations (UN). The United States and its allies had won World War II, and people all over the world wanted to work for peace. Eleanor had the chance to make Franklin's dream come true.

Eleanor served on Committee Three, which dealt with social, educational, and cultural issues. It was the perfect place for her. Eleanor could help make life better for people everywhere.

Eleanor was one of the only female delegates at the first UN meeting.

Once the UN was set up, Eleanor served as the U.S. representative. She also ran the Human Rights Commission. The commission made sure that people around the world could be safe, healthy, and free.

Eleanor led Human Rights Commission meetings. She sometimes kept meetings in order by loudly pounding her gavel—to the surprise of the other delegates.

THE UNIVERSAL DECLARATION OF HUMAN RIGHTS

As the head of the UN Human Rights Commission, Eleanor had a big job. She had to help write an international bill of rights, a set of rights for everyone in all the countries of the world. That took lots of hard work. There were so many ideas among member countries. But Eleanor helped everyone agree. Finally, in 1948, the countries in the UN voted to accept the Universal Declaration of Human Rights.

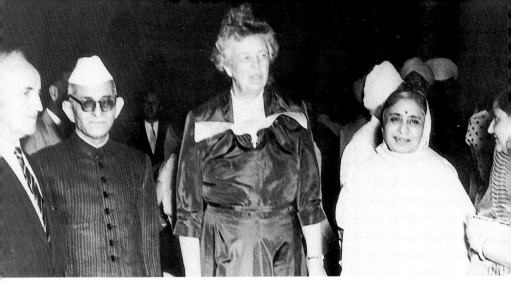

Eleanor stopped in India in 1952 on AAUN business. She met with important government officials there.

In 1952, Eleanor began working for the American Association for the United Nations (AAUN). She traveled around the world to gain support for the UN.

During all this time, Eleanor was still writing her newspaper column three times a week. She also wrote a book about her life, *On My Own,* which came out in 1958.

At the age of seventy-five, Eleanor still kept busy, speaking and writing. In 1960, she wrote another book, called *You Learn by Living.* Eleanor wrote the book in response to the many letters she received from people asking for her advice.

She hosted a television show called *Prospects of Mankind*. Famous people appeared on the show to talk about politics and social issues.

She lectured at Brandeis University, but she didn't want to be called professor. She didn't think she was important enough.

But people all over the country seemed to think Eleanor *was* important. They voted her America's "Most Admired Woman."

At age seventy-seven, Eleanor had her own television show.

Eleanor met with President John F. Kennedy (RIGHT) to discuss the role of women in the government.

In 1961, Eleanor noticed that President John F. Kennedy had chosen few women to work for the government. Eleanor gave Kennedy a three-page list of women she thought could serve in important government jobs.

After that, the president asked her to run the National Commission on the Status of Women. She reported back to Kennedy about the lives of women in the United States. She said she thought men and women deserved equal pay for doing the same job.

Eleanor was as busy as ever, but she tired easily. She had developed a blood disease called aplastic anemia. By the fall of 1962, Eleanor felt weak and confused. She died on November 7, 1962.

Eleanor Roosevelt never thought of herself as special in any way. She just wanted to be useful. She believed that "what one has to do usually can be done."

But Eleanor was far from ordinary. She loved people, and she did her best to help them—rich, poor, black, white, men, women, and children. In her own way, she created a new role for women in the United States. She made a difference.

TIMELINE

In the year . . .

1892	Eleanor's mother died.	Age 8
1893	her brother Ellie died.	
1894	her father died.	
1899	she went to school in England.	
1905	she married Franklin Delano Roosevelt.	Age 20
1906	her first child, Anna, was born.	
1917	the United States joined World War I.	
1919	American women won the right to vote.	
1920	she joined the League of Women Voters.	Age 36
1921	Franklin developed polio.	
1927	she bought Todhunter School.	
1929	the Great Depression began.	
1932	Franklin was elected president.	
1933	she became First Lady. she started building Arthurdale.	Age 49
1935	she started writing her newspaper column.	
1941	the United States entered World War II.	
1943	she visited U.S. troops in the South Pacific.	
1945	Franklin died. World War II ended.	
1946	she started serving in the United Nations.	Age 61
1948	the UN accepted the Universal Declaration of Human Rights.	
1952	she started working for the American Association for the United Nations.	
1961	she began running the Commission on the Status of Women.	
1962	she died on November 7.	Age 78

VAL-KILL

As Eleanor became more involved in her own projects, she found she needed her own place to meet with friends. In 1925, she and her friends Marian Dickerman and Nancy Cook had a cottage built near one of Franklin's family houses. The women named the stone cottage Val-Kill after a nearby stream. Marian and Nancy lived there, and Eleanor stayed there whenever she could.

The three women also started a furniture factory behind the cottage. Nancy ran the factory, and Eleanor helped fund it. After it closed, Eleanor converted it into apartments.

When she left the White House, Eleanor moved to Val-Kill permanently. Eleanor kept very busy there, hosting U.S. and world leaders, family members, and friends.

Since 1977, Val-Kill has been open to visitors who want to see where one of the best-loved First Ladies lived, worked, and played.

FURTHER READING

NONFICTION
Stein, R. Conrad. *The Great Depression.* Chicago: Children's Press, 1993. Explains the causes of the depression, details the troubles faced by millions of Americans, and describes steps taken to get the nation back on its feet.

Whitman, Sylvia. *Children of the World War II Home Front.* Minneapolis: Carolrhoda Books, Inc., 2001. Text and black-and-white photos explore the lives of children and the experiences of families in the United States during World War II.

FICTION
De Young, C. Coco. *A Letter to Mrs. Roosevelt.* New York: Delacorte Press, 1999. It's the Great Depression, and eleven-year-old Margo's family is in danger of losing their house. Margo writes to Eleanor Roosevelt asking for help.

Ryan, Pam Muñoz. *Amelia and Eleanor Go for a Ride.* New York: Scholastic Press, 1999. This picture book is a fictionalized account of what happened on the night in 1933 when famous aviator Amelia Earhart came to dinner at the White House. Eleanor and Amelia went flying together and had a great adventure.

WEBSITES

Dear Mrs. Roosevelt
<http://newdeal.feri.org/eleanor/index.htm> Thousands of children wrote letters to Eleanor when she was First Lady. This website features some of those letters, and it explains what Eleanor did to help children during the Great Depression.

Eleanor Roosevelt National Historical Site
<http://www.nps.gov/elro/> Eleanor's home at Val-Kill is
open to the public. Run by the National Park Service, this
site offers information about the home, as well as facts
about Eleanor's life.

Universal Declaration of Human Rights 50th Anniversary
<http://www.udhr.org/index.htm> This site, run by the
Franklin and Eleanor Roosevelt Institute, offers information
about the Universal Declaration of Human Rights, the
United Nations, and Eleanor's involvement in both.

SELECT BIBLIOGRAPHY

Cook, Blanche Wiesen. *Eleanor Roosevelt: Volume 1,
1884–1933*. New York: Penguin Books, 1992.

Cook, Blanche Wiesen. *Eleanor Roosevelt: Volume 2,
1933–1938*. New York: Viking Penguin, 1999.

Goodwin, Doris Kearns. *No Ordinary Time: Franklin &
Eleanor Roosevelt: The Home Front in World War II*.
New York: Simon & Schuster, 1994.

Lash, Joseph. *Eleanor and Franklin*. New York:
W. W. Norton & Company, 1971.

Lash, Joseph. *Eleanor: The Years Alone*. New York:
W. W. Norton & Company, 1972.

Roosevelt, Eleanor. *The Autobiography of Eleanor
Roosevelt*. New York: Da Capo Press, 1992.

INDEX

Acknowledgments

For photographs: Franklin D. Roosevelt Library, pp. 4, 7, 9, 10, 11, 14, 15, 18, 19, 20, 22, 23, 24, 27, 28, 29, 33, 38, 40, 41, 42; Bureau of Engraving, Washington, D.C., p. 8; © George Eastman House/Lewis W. Hine/Archive Photos, p. 12; © Bettman/CORBIS, p. 31; U.S. Army photograph, p. 34; Franklin D. Roosevelt Library, Photo by George I. Browne, p. 45. Front cover: Douglas Chandor, White House Collection. Back cover: Franklin D. Roosevelt Library.

For quoted material: p. 7, Blanche Wiesen Cook, *Eleanor Roosevelt: Volume 1, 1884–1933* (New York: Penguin Books, 1992); p. 21, Joseph Lash, *Eleanor and Franklin* (New York: W. W. Norton & Company, 1971); p. 36, Doris Kearns Goodwin, *No Ordinary Time: Franklin & Eleanor Roosevelt: The Home Front in World War II* (New York: Simon & Schuster, 1994); p. 43, Eleanor Roosevelt, *The Autobiography of Eleanor Roosevelt* (New York: Da Capo Press, 1992).